To a Wonderful Wom

May God Bless always

Keep you.

All Scripture within this text is drawn from the King James Bible. All rights are subject to Pulic Domain.

This Book in the sole property of To Serve With Love Ministries
ALL Rights Reserved 2007

Teresa Joh
Sept 17-20-10

Table Of Contents

Dedication

Acknowledgements

About To Serve With Love Ministries

Foreword by Pastor Nichica Smith

How To Get The Best Out of Your 365 Day Journal Experience

Let Me Introduce You To Your Lover

Let The Journey Begin

Notes

Calendar

Thank You

Dedication

I dedicate this journal to my Spiritual Father, Bishop Kevin L. Long. You are the best and no one can top that. It was during one of the times that you were sharing with us, your son's and daughter's, about what was in your heart, that you told us to keep a journal and write down things that God will give us. So this is how this journal came about because of you opening your heart to us. I learned to share my heart with others and I learned so much from you. I thank you for birthing me out of the spirit realm. These last three years have been a great joy for me and I have learned so much sitting at your feet. The impartation of your wisdom and the things that you have spoken over my life has helped me to be the person that I am right now. But your love and your walk have been the best of all and I thank you for being such a great example to the body of Christ. I love you so much.

Your Daughter In Christ Jesus,

Teresa Johnson

Acknowledgements

To Serve With Love Ministries would like to thank God for His unconditional love and patience that He shows every day. We thank Him for entrusting us with something so precious and so valuable to the Kingdom. We thank Him for His Word that has kept us and encouraged us daily when we felt like the walls were closing in. We thank Him for the way that He loves us; a way that can never be duplicated or imitated by anything or anyone. He is the ultimate lover and we dedicate not only this journal but our lives to Him!! To Serve With Love Ministries would also like to thank Ms. Lentonia Moye for typing up this journal for us and willingly doing whatever else we have asked you to do.

From The Author:

I would like to take this time to thank everyone that played a part in this journal. To my best friend, my God, my heavenly Father, for giving me the ability to write. Thank you for trusting me.

To my children and grand children, thank you for your support and your love. Linda Thompson, thank you for listening to me when I didn't understand what God was telling me about writing. To my Spiritual Grandparents, Daddy and Mama Long, thank you both for your encouraging words. To my Spiritual Mothers, thank you for your encouraging words and your prayers. To a very special prayer team, Temple Church International, thank you so much for your support. To my prayer partner Tammie, thank you for being my friend in a hard time and for praying for me. I know when I wanted to give up, it was you calling and talking to me that helped. To Pastor Nichica Smith, thank you for all your support and love. I will not forget. To Pastor Robyn Gool of Victory Christian Center thank you for teaching me how to speak the Word of God over my life. To Donna Ossorio and Venessa Cannady, thank you for your listening ear and your words of encouragement. To the Water Walker's Summit Advisory Council, thank you for your hard work and dedication. And to the parents of To Serve With Love Academy, thank you all. Special thank you to the Temple Church International Ministerial Staff for your love and support. And to my brothers and sisters in Christ: Joseph Bennett, Selena Bennett, Brian and Sheila Villegas, Pamela Massey, Ramondez and Niki Grier, Angela Lipscomb, Pat Singleton, Tim and Angie Grier, thank you all for being in my life. To the Water Walker team, thank you all for your support and love.

To My Administrator, Pastor Nichica Smith

I thank God for you and the gift that you are. From my heart I thank you so much for being here for me during the good times and bad. The words that come out of my mouth come from my heart and I want you to know that I could not have done this without you. I am grateful to God the Father that He saw that I needed some help and not just any kind of help, but the right kind of help. I thank you for answering the call from God and I pray that God will always bless you for showing your labor of love and support.

Thank you always,

About To Serve With Love Ministries, Inc.

To Serve With Love Ministries, under the Apostolic covering of Bishop Kevin L. Long, started out as a one room home daycare in Charlotte, NC and at that time was called To Serve With Love House of Learning. In 2001 the prophecy we received from Bishop Kevin L. Long changed the life of To Serve With Love. At that time he did not know Minister Johnson or the work she did. He said that To Serve With Love House of Learning would no longer be a daycare, but a ministry that would touch people from all walks of life. It was at that time that the enemy tried everything to stop the vision, but God saw fit to send different people to help Minister Johnson.

To Serve With Love Ministries is an outreach ministry that ministers to the entire family. The following ministries make up To Serve With Love Ministries:

    To Serve With Love Academy: for children ages 6wks through 12th grade
    House of Refuge: offers temporary housing, job training, job placement, life skills to displaced families and individuals
    Cornerstone: offers life skills training for youth and young adults through Age 21
    Water Walker's Summit: education and empowerment of the entire family through the unadulterated Word of God.
    Beat The Odds Foundation: provide scholarships to displaced individuals seeking to further their education

Covenant Partners: our covenant partners are the backbone of this ministry by sowing their time, talent, and financial resources that we can help anyone that wants our help. Our covenant partners receive special gifts and discounts as a thank you for their dedication to the vision.

24 Hour Prayer Line: toll free number where people can call in from all over the world and request prayer.

    To Serve With Love Ministries is about Kingdom building and being an extended arm to pastors. If you would like to know more about the ministry or desire to become a Covenant Partner, please feel free to contact the ministry via our website at www.toservewithloveministries.com.

Foreword by Pastor Nichica Smith

When one thinks of intimacy the first thought is the sexual encounter between two individuals. However, it is that course of thinking that has prevented so many from experiencing intimacy versus having intimacy. An experience usually happens over a period of time, but you can have something today and lose it tomorrow. However intimacy is defined as the emotional bond we share, a feeling of deep connection, secure attachment and belonging. Intimacy helps to bring about a oneness which is why so many people long for it, but go about it the wrong way.

One does not know love until they know the love of God and one has not experienced true intimacy until they experience it with God. He is the master teacher, master friend, and master lover. He fills every void in our lives IF we allow Him to. He is the perfect gentleman and will never force Himself on anyone. But if you tell Him 'yes' and mean it, the experience will be one that you will never forget and the love you receive will be something that you will never want to be without.

Minister Teresa Johnson, out of her own yearning and aching for that special 'something' in her life, allowed God to teach her how to be loved and more importantly how to be loved by Him. She allowed God to be the lover of her heart, mind, body, and soul.

Understand that God is not looking for a one night stand and neither is He looking for an on and off relationship. He is looking to give His all to you if you are willing to give your all to Him. Don't allow past hurts and disappointments stop you from getting what you have been crying out for. Don't allow the enemy to rob you of another second of real love…real intimacy! I encourage you right now, men and women of God whether you are seasoned or a babe in Christ. The best is yet to come, but it will start with your willingness to let go and embark on the experience of intimacy that this journal has to offer. I know that as you are reading this foreword, that God is speaking to your heart and you feel His presence even now. Imagine what the rest will be like!

Enjoy!!!

Get the Best Out of Your 365 Day Journal

When we think about the word intimate, there are different adjectives that come to mind. Some of them include special, cherished, personal, profound, and in-depth. You are about to embark on a journey that is going to take you right to the heart of God. A journey so powerful, that your very life will change forever.

Have you ever wanted to be in the presence of God? Have you ever wanted to tap into the manifest presence of God? If so, then prepare yourself to receive just that by opening up your mind, heart, and spirit to what is on the subsequent pages of this journal. This is your intimate time with God, so please write down what He is saying and how you are feeling. Be sure to write down the dates and include the year so that you can go back and reflect on how God has moved in your life and the things He was preparing you for. Once you have been intimate with the Father, you will know that there is nothing in the world like it and there never will be. So get ready as you spend not just the next 365 days with God, but the rest of your life!!

This is how it works:

1. For each month there is an overall theme that you should keep at the forefront of your mind.

2. For each week there is a scripture for you to meditate on and then write your thoughts or reflections down for each day of the week as God gives it to you. These thoughts may come while you are driving, while you are washing the dishes, or mowing the lawn. Do not discount even the simplest thought as God is not complicated.

3. There is a prayer at the end of each week that you must say out loud. However this prayer is not to be said only at the end of the week, it is a prayer that you need to say everyday after you write your reflection for that day.

4. At the very back of the journal are empty pages that you should use to write down promises or visions that God gives you. You should write down the date that He gave it to you and also the date that it came to pass. You should also write down things that you would like God to do in your life and things that you would like God to make clearer or provide clarity on. These could be things in your life or something you read in His word. Again, write the date that the request was made and the date that it was answered.

    If you do everything just as indicated, by the end of the year you will be higher in the Lord and closer to Him than you ever thought could be possible. My prayers are with you and so is the spirit of the living God……enjoy your journey!

(All scriptures come from the New King James Version)

Let Me Introduce You To Your Lover..........

Have you ever wanted to be in the presence of someone that loved you just for you? They didn't care about the color of your skin, the length of your hair, or how many degrees you have. Someone that you could talk to in the morning, noon, or night and they would be attentive and hang on your every word. Have you ever wanted to know what it felt like to be truly loved by someone and to experience a connection that could not severed? Have you ever told yourself that you were tired of foolishness and you wanted something real this time?

What if I told that you didn't have to go to the websites, the bars, the dating clubs, etc? What if I told that what you were looking for was right there under your nose, waiting with just as much anticipation as you? What if I told you all you had to do was say, "Yes", and invite Him into your heart? Would you believe me? Well, let me tell you a little about Him, before I introduce you to Him. He is everything anyone could hope for. He has understanding that no one could even dare try to match. He has a love that has yet to be beat by anything or anyone. Once you are in His presence, your very life changes. To walk with Him, is to be engulfed in eternal satisfaction. He covers you with an impenetrable covering and His words are a calming influence to your very soul.

So how can you meet Him……by taking an unforgettable journey. We have tried to make it easier by providing you with this journal, as we know that first experiences and rekindling of love are hard to initiate. Now this is not the kind of journal you can read from page to page and if you try to you will miss the experience of a life time……..intimacy with your lover. The impact that He wants to make in your life and in your heart is like nothing you will ever experience from another being as long you live. In your quality time with Him you will find yourself refreshed, rejuvenated, revived, and restored to the fullest and just when you think you have experienced His best…..He surprises you by taking you higher in Him.

The Bible tells us that God is love (I John 4:16) and to be intimate with Him is simply to experience Him in His glory. And once you experience Him, it creates an insatiable thirst that can only be quenched by God, the Father. And no matter where we go, or how often we might stray, we are always drawn back to Him…the one that gave us true intimacy. This experience with your lover will help you to be honest about where you are in your walk with Him and ultimately confident about your love with and for God. You have the ability to love Him and be loved by Him at any point of the day or night; this journal will help you tap into the desire to want to love Him and be loved by Him.

So now, let me introduce you to your lover…………………………………..

Falling In Love With Jesus; Having His Heart

      Falling in love is a scary thing for most people because they don't know what to expect and at times it seems too risky. They are worried about whether or not the other person will give as much as they will or they wonder if the other person will love them the way they deserve and desire to be loved. LEAVE ALL OF THAT BEHIND!!!!

      God created you. The Bible reminds us that He knew you before you were even born into this Earth. Not only can He love you the way you want to be loved, but He will give more than you could ever ask for. Just open your heart and allow the courtship to begin. I know it sounds like I am asking you to jump off a cliff and take a deep plunge and you are partly right. I am asking you to take a deep plunge, but one that you will not regret. It was hard for me at first to allow myself to fall in love with Jesus and to believe all that was said about Him. The reason that it was hard was because I desired a physical interaction, I wanted someone that I could see, feel, hear, and touch and I did not believe that Jesus could give me that. Don't be the fool that I was. I waited until I was shattered, angry, resentful, and had so many walls built up around me because of people that had used and abused me that Jesus was my last hope when He should have been my first choice. There are times when I am busy doing something, anything and I feel His presence and it engulfs me to the point that I don't want to do anything but focus on Him. There are times when I breathe in and I can smell His sweet aroma all around me and there are times when I hear Him whisper to me the words that always put a smile on my face I Love You!

      Now I didn't get to this overnight, but I give Him glory that I am there now because what I have with Him is nothing short of IMMACULATE and the wonderful thing is…..you can have it to!

Falling in Love with God; Having his Heart

Week 1. Read Romans 5:1-5

Therefore having been justified by faith we have peace with God through our Lord Jesus Christ through whom also we have access by faith into this grace in which we stand and rejoice in hope of the glory of God and not only that but we also have glory in tribulation. Know that tribulation produces perseverance, perseverance produces character, and character produces hope. Now hope does not disappoint, because the love of God has been poured out in our heart by the Holy Spirit who was given to us.

Sunday's Reflections

Date_____

Journal _____
_____
_____
_____
_____

Monday's Reflections

Date_____

Journal _____
_____
_____
_____
_____

Tuesday's Reflections

Date_____

Journal _____
_____
_____
_____
_____

Wednesday's Reflections

Date_____

Journal _____
_____
_____
_____
_____

Thursday's Reflections

Date_____

Journal _____
_____
_____
_____
_____

Friday's Reflections

Date_____

Journal _____
_____
_____
_____
_____

Saturday's Reflections

Date_____

Journal _____
_____
_____
_____
_____

Week 2. Read Jeremiah 17:9-11

The heart is deceitful above all things and desperately wicked; who can know it? I, the Lord, search the heart, I test the mind, Even to give every man according to his ways, according to the fruit of his doings. As a partridge that broods but does not hatch, So is he who gets riches but not by right; it will leave him in the midst of his days and at his end he will be a fool.

Sunday's Reflections

Date _____

Journal _____
_____
_____
_____
_____

Monday's Reflections

Date _____

Journal _____
_____
_____
_____
_____

Tuesday's Reflections

Date _____

Journal _____
_____
_____
_____
_____

Wednesday's Reflections

Date _____

Journal _____
_____
_____
_____
_____

Thursday's Reflections

Date_____

Journal _____
_____
_____
_____

Friday's Reflections

Date_____

Journal _____
_____
_____
_____

Saturday's Reflections

Date_____

Journal _____
_____
_____
_____

Week 3. Read Joshua 22:5 & Matthew 22:37

But take careful heed to do the commandment and the law which Moses the servant of the Lord commanded you to love the Lord your God, to walk in all his ways to keep his commandments, to hold fast to Him, and to serve Him with all your heart and with all your soul. Jesus said to him, You shall love the Lord your God with all your heart, with all your soul, and with all your mind.

Sunday's Reflections

Date_____

Journal _____
_____
_____
_____
_____

Monday's Reflections

Date_____

Journal _____
_____
_____
_____
_____

Tuesday's Reflections

Date_____

Journal _____
_____
_____
_____
_____

Wednesday's Reflections

Date_____

Journal _____
_____
_____
_____
_____

Thursday's Reflections

Date _____

Journal _____
_____
_____
_____
_____

Friday's Reflections

Date _____

Journal _____
_____
_____
_____
_____

Saturday's Reflections

Date _____

Journal _____
_____
_____
_____
_____

Week 4. Read Genesis 6: 4-7

There were giants on the earth in those days and also afterward when the sons of God came in to the daughters of men and they bore children to them. Those were the mighty men who were of old, men of renown. Then the Lord saw that the wickedness of man was great in the earth and that every intent of the thoughts of his heart was only evil continually. And the Lord was sorry that He had made man on the earth and He was grieved in His heart.

Sunday's Reflections

Date_____

Journal _____
_____
_____
_____
_____

Monday's Reflections

Date_____

Journal _____
_____
_____
_____
_____

Tuesday's Reflections

Date_____

Journal _____
_____
_____
_____
_____

Wednesday's Reflections

Date_____

Journal _____
_____
_____
_____
_____

Thursday's Reflections

Date _____

Journal _____
_____
_____
_____
_____

Friday's Reflections

Date _____

Journal _____
_____
_____
_____
_____

Saturday's Reflections

Date _____

Journal _____
_____
_____
_____
_____

Week 5. Read 1 Samuel 1: 12-13, 1 Samuel 2:1

And it happened as she continued praying before the Lord that Eli watched her mouth. Now Hannah spoke in her heart; only her lips moved but her voice was not heard. And Hannah prayed and said: My heart rejoices in the Lord; My horn is exalted in the Lord. I smile at my enemies, Because I rejoice in Your salvation.

Sunday's Reflections

Date_____

Journal _____
_____
_____
_____
_____

Monday's Reflections

Date_____

Journal _____
_____
_____
_____
_____

Tuesday's Reflections

Date_____

Journal _____
_____
_____
_____
_____

Wednesday's Reflections

Date_____

Journal _____
_____
_____
_____
_____

Thursday's Reflections

Date _____

Journal _____
_____
_____
_____
_____

Friday's Reflections

Date _____

Journal _____
_____
_____
_____
_____

Saturday's Reflections

Date _____

Journal _____
_____
_____
_____
_____

Prayer

Father, in the name of Jesus, I ask you right now to search my heart and reveal to me anything that may be hidden and not of you. It is my desire that you fill my heart with your love, patience, and forgiveness. I praise you everyday that you decided to love me in spite of my many faults and that you have a special place in your heart for me. Amen.

(Now go to the back of the journal and record what God has spoken, the date He spoke it, and when the manifestation of God's promise is revealed; record it in the journal. Go through this process for each week so that the reminder and the remembrance of God's unchanging word is ever before you.)

Seek The Lord

      We all have been guilty of looking for love in all the wrong places and in all the wrong things. But can you honestly say that you ever looked for those things in God? More than likely, the answer is no. And if you did, did you allow Him to do what He does best?

      To seek something is to look for it with a fervent desire and you don't stop until you find it. The Bible tells us that if we seek we shall find, if we ask it shall be given unto us, and if we knock it shall be opened unto us. Therefore seek the Lord, ask Him to be your all and all, and knock on the doors of His heart.

      Don't be concerned with the opinions of others and whether or not they will understand or whether or not they will appreciate it enough to encourage you. I have constantly looked for the approval of others and the encouragement of others because I always gave the encouragement to people who needed it. But when I needed it and did not receive it, I would be angry, hurt, and frustrated because we all want to be encouraged and we all want to be loved. Understand my beloved, stop looking for people to constantly give you things that God has already spoken that He will provide. When you consistently seek the Lord and all of His righteousness, you will find that you are no longer running on empty and the thirst that you had is being quenched. God is not a man that He should lie as He can't lie. Everything you need is in God, but you have to seek it out and ask Him for it and the greatest thing is that He will not withhold Himself from you. I have made a lot of mistakes in my life, but seeking the Lord has never been one of them and it won't be one of yours either.

February

Seek the Lord

Week 1. Read 1 Chronicles 16: 10-11

Glory in His holy name. Let the hearts of those rejoice who seek the Lord! Seek the Lord and His strength. Seek his face evermore!

Sunday's Reflections

Date_____

Journal _____
_____
_____
_____

Monday's Reflections

Date_____

Journal _____
_____
_____
_____

Tuesday's Reflections

Date_____

Journal _____
_____
_____
_____

Wednesday's Reflections

Date_____

Journal _____
_____
_____
_____

Thursday's Reflections

Date_____

Journal _____
_____
_____
_____
_____

Friday's Reflections

Date_____

Journal _____
_____
_____
_____
_____

Saturday's Reflections

Date_____

Journal _____
_____
_____
_____
_____

Week 2. Read 1 Chronicles 22:19

Now set your heart and your soul to seek the Lord your God. Therefore arise and build the sanctuary of the Lord God to bring the ark of the covenant of the Lord and the holy articles of God into the house that is to be built for the name of the Lord.

Sunday's Reflections

Date_____

Journal _____
_____
_____
_____
_____

Monday's Reflections

Date_____

Journal _____
_____
_____
_____
_____

Tuesday's Reflections

Date_____

Journal _____
_____
_____
_____
_____

Wednesday's Reflections

Date_____

Journal _____
_____
_____
_____
_____

Thursday's Reflections

Date_____

Journal _____
_____
_____
_____

Friday's Reflections

Date_____

Journal _____
_____
_____
_____

Saturday's Reflections

Date_____

Journal _____
_____
_____
_____

Week 3. Read 2 Chronicles 11: 16-17

And after the Levites left those from all the tribes of Israel such as set their heart to seek Lord God of Israel came to Jerusalem to sacrifice to the Lord God of their father.
So they strengthened the kingdom of Judah and made Rehoboam the son of Solomon strong for three years, because they walked in the way of David and Solomon for three years.

Sunday's Reflections

Date_____

Journal _____
_____
_____
_____

Monday's Reflections

Date_____

Journal _____
_____
_____
_____

Tuesday's Reflections

Date_____

Journal _____
_____
_____
_____

Wednesday's Reflections

Date_____

Journal _____
_____
_____
_____

Thursday's Reflections

Date _____

Journal _____
_____
_____
_____
_____

Friday's Reflections

Date _____

Journal _____
_____
_____
_____
_____

Saturday's Reflections

Date _____

Journal _____
_____
_____
_____
_____

Week 4. Read Psalm 105:4; Psalm 34:8-12

Seek the Lord and his strength, seek his face evermore!
Oh taste and see that the Lord is good. Blessed is the man who trusts in him! Oh fear the Lord you His saints! There is no want to those who fear Him. The young lions lack and suffer hunger; but those who seek the Lord shall not lack any good thing. Come, you children, listen to me; I will teach you the fear of the Lord. Who is the man who desires life, and loves many days, that he may see goods?

Sunday's Reflections

Date_____

Journal _____
_____
_____
_____
_____

Monday's Reflections

Date_____

Journal _____
_____
_____
_____
_____

Tuesday's Reflections

Date_____

Journal _____
_____
_____
_____
_____

Wednesday's Reflections

Date_____

Journal _____
_____
_____
_____
_____

Thursday's Reflections

Date_____

Journal _____
_____
_____
_____
_____

Friday's Reflections

Date_____

Journal _____
_____
_____
_____
_____

Saturday's Reflections

Date_____

Journal _____
_____
_____
_____
_____

Week 5. Read Ezra 6:21-22

Then the children of Israel who had returned from the captivity ate together with all who had separated themselves from the filth of the nations of the land in order to seek the Lord God of Israel. And they kept the Feast of Unleavened Bread seven days with joy; for the Lord made them joyful and turned the heart of the king of Assyria toward them, to strengthen their hands in the work of the house of God, the God of Israel.

Sunday's Reflections

Date_____

Journal _____
_____
_____
_____
_____

Monday's Reflections

Date_____

Journal _____
_____
_____
_____
_____

Tuesday's Reflections

Date_____

Journal _____
_____
_____
_____
_____

Wednesday's Reflections

Date_____

Journal _____
_____
_____
_____
_____

Thursday's Reflections

Date_____

Journal _____
_____
_____
_____
_____

Friday's Reflections

Date_____

Journal _____
_____
_____
_____
_____

Saturday's Reflections

Date_____

Journal _____
_____
_____
_____
_____

Prayer

Lord, you know just how rebellious I have been. I ask your forgiveness for manipulating circumstances and people. I ask that you forgive me for trying to manipulate you to get my own way. May your will be done in my life, even as it is in heaven.

(Now go to the back of the journal and record what God has spoken, the date He spoke it, and when the manifestation of God's promise is revealed; record it in the journal. Go through this process for each week so that the reminder and the remembrance of God's unchanging word is ever before you.)

Humble Yourself

It is hard to deal with someone else's ego. The arrogance that some can portray can make you not want to be around them at all. However when we declare that we are in love, we should want to establish a mood for our lover. The mood can not be set, nor can you be received until you humble yourself.

Humbling oneself does not mean that you degrade yourself or become less than what God has created you to be. In fact, what it means is that you allow God to love the way that He can love you. You don't dictate to Him what the experience must be like, how long it needs to last, where it needs to take place, or when it needs to take place. What you do is literally say," Lord I am yours and I open myself to be loved by you because I trust you and my faith is in you. You have never failed me and I know every moment with you is better than the last so love me Lord the way you see fit and I am ready to receive your best."

We don't like to be bossed around and neither does God, so be humble and be ready!

March

Humble Yourself

Week 1. Read Luke 15:18-19

I will arise and go to my father, and will say to him, "Father, I have sinned against heaven and before you, and I am no longer worthy to be called your son. Make me like one of your hired servants."

Sunday's Reflections

Date_____

Journal _____
_____
_____
_____
_____

Monday's Reflections

Date_____

Journal _____
_____
_____
_____
_____

Tuesday's Reflections

Date_____

Journal _____
_____
_____
_____
_____

Wednesday's Reflections

Date_____

Journal _____
_____
_____
_____
_____

Thursday's Reflections

Date_____

Journal _____
_____
_____
_____
_____

Friday's Reflections

Date_____

Journal _____
_____
_____
_____
_____

Saturday's Reflections

Date_____

Journal _____
_____
_____
_____
_____

Week 2. Read 2 Chronicles 33:12-13

Now when he was in affliction, he implored the Lord his God and humbled himself greatly before the God of his fathers, and prayed to him and he received his entreaty, heard his supplication, and brought him back to Jerusalem into his kingdom. Then Manasseh knew that the Lord was God.

Sunday's Reflections

Date_____

Journal _____
_____
_____
_____
_____

Monday's Reflections

Date_____

Journal _____
_____
_____
_____
_____

Tuesday's Reflections

Date_____

Journal _____
_____
_____
_____
_____

Wednesday's Reflections

Date_____

Journal _____
_____
_____
_____
_____

Thursday's Reflections

Date_____

Journal _____
_____
_____
_____
_____

Friday's Reflections

Date_____

Journal _____
_____
_____
_____
_____

Saturday's Reflections

Date_____

Journal _____
_____
_____
_____
_____

Week 3. Read Philippians 2:5-8

Let this mind be in you which was also in Christ Jesus, who being in the form of God, did not consider it robbery to be equal with God, but made himself of no reputation, taking the form of a bond servant and coming in the likeness of men. And being found in appearance as a man, He humbled Himself and became obedient to the point of death, even the death of the cross.

Sunday's Reflections

Date_____

Journal _____
_____
_____
_____
_____

Monday's Reflections

Date_____

Journal _____
_____
_____
_____
_____

Tuesday's Reflections

Date_____

Journal _____
_____
_____
_____
_____

Wednesday's Reflections

Date_____

Journal _____
_____
_____
_____
_____

Thursday's Reflections

Date_____

Journal _____
_____
_____
_____
_____

Friday's Reflections

Date_____

Journal _____
_____
_____
_____
_____

Saturday's Reflections

Date_____

Journal _____
_____
_____
_____
_____

Week 4. Read Psalm 113:6-9

Who humbles himself to behold the things that are in the heavens and in the earth? He raises the poor out of the dust, and lifts the needy out of the ash heap that He may seat him with princes, with the princes of his people. He grants the barren woman a home like a joyful mother of children.

Sunday's Reflections

Date_____

Journal _____
_____
_____
_____
_____

Monday's Reflections

Date_____

Journal _____
_____
_____
_____
_____

Tuesday's Reflections

Date_____

Journal _____
_____
_____
_____
_____

Wednesday's Reflections

Date_____

Journal _____
_____
_____
_____
_____

Thursday's Reflections

Date_____

Journal _____
_____
_____
_____
_____

Friday's Reflections

Date_____

Journal _____
_____
_____
_____
_____

Saturday's Reflections

Date_____

Journal _____
_____
_____
_____
_____

Week 5. Read Psalm 123:1-2

Unto you I lift up my eyes, O you who dwell in the heavens. Behold, as the eyes of servants look to the hand of their masters, as the eyes of a maid to the hand of her mistress, so our eyes look to the Lord Our God, until he has mercy on us.

Sunday's Reflections

Date_____

Journal _____
_____
_____
_____
_____

Monday's Reflections

Date_____

Journal _____
_____
_____
_____
_____

Tuesday's Reflections

Date_____

Journal _____
_____
_____
_____
_____

Wednesday's Reflections

Date_____

Journal _____
_____
_____
_____
_____

Thursday's Reflections

Date_____

Journal _____
_____
_____
_____
_____

Friday's Reflections

Date_____

Journal _____
_____
_____
_____
_____

Saturday's Reflections

Date_____

Journal _____
_____
_____
_____
_____

Prayer

Father, I come to you in the name of Jesus. With the help of the Holy Spirit and by your grace, I join with the heavenly host making a joyful noise to you and serving you with gladness. I come before your presence with singing. Lord I know, recognize, and understand with approval that you are God! It is you who made us and not we ourselves and we are yours; we are your people and the sheep of your pasture. I humble myself before your throne, that you may have your way in and through my life.

(Now go to the back of the journal and record what God has spoken, the date He spoke it, and when the manifestation of God's promise is revealed; record it in the journal. Go through this process for each week so that the reminder and the remembrance of God's unchanging word is ever before you.)

Humility

One trait that we detest in our lover is inconsistency. It is difficult to deal with a person whose personality and behavior changes from one minute to the next. In order to experience true intimacy with your lover, humility and humbleness must be an everyday part of who you are. The Bible tells us that God is the same yesterday, today, and forever; don't we owe our lover the same respect?

As we are eagerly seeking for God to give us what we need, it is important to remember that this is a two way street. We have all been on the receiving end of someone who always wanted to take and not give back. Sooner or later you were depleted and miserable because you gave someone all that you had and they gave nothing back in return. Don't do this to God and if you are unsure as to how to have humility and to be respectful, then let God teach you. Remember He is the Master teacher and I can testify to you on today that God is gentle, He is patient, and He is kind and as long as you don't give up on Him….He will never give up on YOU!

April

Humility

Week 1. Read 1 Peter 5: 5-7

Likewise you younger people, submit yourselves to your elders, yes all of you be submissive to one another and be clothed with humility, for God resists the proud but gives grace to the humble. Therefore humble yourselves under the mighty hand of God that he may exalt you in due time, casting all your care upon Him, for he cares for you.

Sunday's Reflections

Date_____

Journal _____
_____
_____
_____
_____

Monday's Reflections

Date_____

Journal _____
_____
_____
_____
_____

Tuesday's Reflections

Date_____

Journal _____
_____
_____
_____
_____

Wednesday's Reflections

Date_____

Journal _____
_____
_____
_____
_____

Thursday's Reflections

Date_____

Journal _____
_____
_____
_____
_____

Friday's Reflections

Date_____

Journal _____
_____
_____
_____
_____

Saturday's Reflections

Date_____

Journal _____
_____
_____
_____
_____

Week 2. Read Proverbs 22: 4-5

By humility and the fear of the Lord are riches and honor and life. Thorns and snares are in the way of the perverse. He who guards his soul will be far from them.

Sunday's Reflections

Date _____

Journal _____
_____
_____
_____
_____

Monday's Reflections

Date _____

Journal _____
_____
_____
_____
_____

Tuesday's Reflections

Date _____

Journal _____
_____
_____
_____
_____

Wednesday's Reflections

Date _____

Journal _____
_____
_____
_____
_____

Thursday's Reflections

Date_____

Journal _____
_____
_____
_____
_____

Friday's Reflections

Date_____

Journal _____
_____
_____
_____
_____

Saturday's Reflections

Date_____

Journal _____
_____
_____
_____
_____

Week 3. Read Colossians 3:12-13

Therefore, as the elect of God, holy and beloved, put on tender mercies, kindness, humility, meekness, and longsuffering; bearing with one another, and forgiving one another, if anyone has a complaint against another; even as Christ forgave you so you also must do.

Sunday's Reflections

Date_____

Journal _____
_____
_____
_____
_____

Monday's Reflections

Date_____

Journal _____
_____
_____
_____
_____

Tuesday's Reflections

Date_____

Journal _____
_____
_____
_____
_____

Wednesday's Reflections

Date_____

Journal _____
_____
_____
_____
_____

Thursday's Reflections

Date_____

Journal _____
_____
_____
_____
_____

Friday's Reflections

Date_____

Journal _____
_____
_____
_____
_____

Saturday's Reflections

Date_____

Journal _____
_____
_____
_____
_____

Week 4. Read Psalm 119:11-12

Your word I have hidden in my heart that I might not sin against You. Blessed are You, O Lord! Teach me your statutes.

Sunday's Reflections

Date_____

Journal _____
_____
_____
_____
_____

Monday's Reflections

Date_____

Journal _____
_____
_____
_____
_____

Tuesday's Reflections

Date_____

Journal _____
_____
_____
_____
_____

Wednesday's Reflections

Date_____

Journal _____
_____
_____
_____
_____

Thursday's Reflections

Date_____

Journal _____
_____
_____
_____
_____

Friday's Reflections

Date_____

Journal _____
_____
_____
_____
_____

Saturday's Reflections

Date_____

Journal _____
_____
_____
_____
_____

Week 5. Read Zephaniah 2:3

Seek the Lord, all you meek of the earth, who have upheld His justice. Seek righteousness, seek humility. It may be that you will be hidden in the day of the Lord's anger.

Sunday's Reflections

Date_____

Journal _____
_____
_____
_____

Monday's Reflections

Date_____

Journal _____
_____
_____
_____

Tuesday's Reflections

Date_____

Journal _____
_____
_____
_____

Wednesday's Reflections

Date_____

Journal _____
_____
_____
_____

Thursday's Reflections

Date_____

Journal _____
_____
_____
_____
_____

Friday's Reflections

Date_____

Journal _____
_____
_____
_____
_____

Saturday's Reflections

Date_____

Journal _____
_____
_____
_____
_____

Father I humble myself and submit to your word that speaks, exposes, sifts, analyzes, and judges the very thoughts and purposes of my heart. I know that I do not always display a spirit of meekness, so God I ask you to forgive me for my arrogance and impatience. I know your way is perfect and I desire to walk the path that you have laid out for me with a meek and humble heart, mind, and spirit.

(Now go to the back of the journal and record what God has spoken, the date He spoke it, and when the manifestation of God's promise is revealed; record it in the journal. Go through this process for each week so that the reminder and the remembrance of God's unchanging word is ever before you.)

Conquering The Thought Life

We all know that the mind is extremely powerful and it directs and guides us through different situations and circumstances. However, when we have been with our lover we know that we must keep our minds stayed on Him and bring everything under subjection to His will and His purpose. If we do this, He has promised us that He will keep us in perfect peace.

Peace……..doesn't that sound wonderful?! But it isn't always the easiest thing to maintain given the world that we are in. However, you can chaos going on around you and have peace on the inside of you and that is what you want to ultimately achieve. We can not control everything in this world, but we can control what we allow to have influence over us. Let God be that influence and let this experience be a constant reminder that through God, the love of God, and the love for God, my mind can be at peace and so can everything in my life.

It was through the mind that everything was created as when God thought it, He spoke it, and it was so. So imagine what He has already thought of for you! Hmmmm…ain't God good!

May

Conquering the Thought Life

Week 1. Read 2 Corinthians 10:3-6

For though we walk in the flesh, we do not war according to the flesh. For the weapons of our warfare are not carnal but mighty in God for pulling down strongholds, casting down arguments and every high thing that exalts itself against the knowledge of God bringing every thought into captivity to the obedience of Christ and being ready to punish all disobedience when your obedience is fulfilled.

Sunday's Reflections

Date_____

Journal _____
_____
_____
_____
_____

Monday's Reflections

Date_____

Journal _____
_____
_____
_____
_____

Tuesday's Reflections

Date_____

Journal _____
_____
_____
_____
_____

Wednesday's Reflections

Date_____

Journal _____
_____
_____
_____
_____

Thursday's Reflections

Date_____

Journal _____
_____
_____
_____
_____

Friday's Reflections

Date_____

Journal _____
_____
_____
_____
_____

Saturday's Reflections

Date_____

Journal _____
_____
_____
_____
_____

Week 2. Read Psalm 103: 1-5

Bless the Lord O my soul, and all that is within me bless His holy name! Bless the Lord, O my soul, and forget not all His benefits who forgives all your iniquities, who heals all your diseases who redeems life from destruction, who crowns you with loving kindness and tender mercies, who satisfies your mouth with good things so that your youth is renewed like the eagles.

Sunday's Reflections

Date_____

Journal _____
_____
_____
_____
_____

Monday's Reflections

Date_____

Journal _____
_____
_____
_____
_____

Tuesday's Reflections

Date_____

Journal _____
_____
_____
_____
_____

Wednesday's Reflections

Date_____

Journal _____
_____
_____
_____
_____

Thursday's Reflections

Date_____

Journal _____
_____
_____
_____
_____

Friday's Reflections

Date_____

Journal _____
_____
_____
_____
_____

Saturday's Reflections

Date_____

Journal _____
_____
_____
_____
_____

Week 3. Read 1 Peter 1: 12-13

To them it was revealed that, not to themselves, but to us they were ministering the things which now have been reported to you through those who have preached the gospel to you by the Holy Spirit sent from heaven things which angels desire to look into. Therefore gird up the lions of your mind, be sober, and rest your hope fully upon the grace that is to be brought to you at revelation of Jesus Christ.

Sunday's Reflections

Date_____

Journal _____
_____
_____
_____
_____

Monday's Reflections

Date_____

Journal _____
_____
_____
_____
_____

Tuesday's Reflections

Date_____

Journal _____
_____
_____
_____
_____

Wednesday's Reflections

Date_____

Journal _____
_____
_____
_____
_____

Thursday's Reflections

Date_____

Journal _____
_____
_____
_____
_____

Friday's Reflections

Date_____

Journal _____
_____
_____
_____
_____

Saturday's Reflections

Date_____

Journal _____
_____
_____
_____
_____

Week 4. Read Colossians 3: 1-4

If then you were raised with Christ, seek those things which are above, where Christ is, sitting at the right hand of God. Set your mind on things above, not on things on the earth. For you died, and your life is hidden with Christ in God. When Christ who is our life appears, then you also will appear with Him in glory.

Sunday's Reflections

Date_____

Journal _____
_____
_____
_____
_____

Monday's Reflections

Date_____

Journal _____
_____
_____
_____
_____

Tuesday's Reflections

Date_____

Journal _____
_____
_____
_____
_____

Wednesday's Reflections

Date_____

Journal _____
_____
_____
_____
_____

Thursday's Reflections

Date_____

Journal _____
_____
_____
_____
_____

Friday's Reflections

Date_____

Journal _____
_____
_____
_____
_____

Saturday's Reflections

Date_____

Journal _____
_____
_____
_____
_____

Week 5. Read Philippians 4:8-9

Finally, brethren whatever things are true, whatever things are noble, whatever things are just, whatever things are pure, whatever things are lovely, whatever things are of good report, if there is any virtue and if there is anything praise worthy- meditate on these things. The things, which you learned and received and heard and saw in me, these do, and the God of peace will be with you.

Sunday's Reflections

Date_____

Journal _____
_____
_____
_____
_____

Monday's Reflections

Date_____

Journal _____
_____
_____
_____
_____

Tuesday's Reflections

Date_____

Journal _____
_____
_____
_____
_____

Wednesday's Reflections

Date_____

Journal _____
_____
_____
_____
_____

Thursday's Reflections

Date_____

Journal _____
_____
_____
_____
_____

Friday's Reflections

Date_____

Journal _____
_____
_____
_____
_____

Saturday's Reflections

Date_____

Journal _____
_____
_____
_____
_____

Prayer

Father God in the name of Jesus Christ I take authority over my thought life. Even though I walk in the flesh I am not carrying on my warfare according to the flesh. For the weapons of my warfare are not physical weapons of flesh and blood; but they are mighty before God for the overthrow and destruction of strongholds. I come against every proud and lofty thing that set itself up against the triune. I test my own actions, so that I might have appropriate self-esteem without comparing myself to anyone else. I lead every thought and purpose away captive into obedience of Christ the anointed one. The security of your guidance will allow me to carry my own load with energy and confidence.

(Now go to the back of the journal and record what God has spoken, the date He spoke it, and when the manifestation of God's promise is revealed; record it in the journal. Go through this process for each week so that the reminder and the remembrance of God's unchanging word is ever before you.)

Righteousness of God

God has an essence and an aura that is pure to the core and everything about Him is pure and holy. Righteousness can be explained and defined in several ways, but the only perfect example is God. Let Him be your example and your guide now and forever.

You may be struggling right now saying God I can't be who you want me to be, I just don't have it in me to do that. What you need to do right now is stop because you have entertained the lies of the enemy and therefore you have allowed poison to enter in. To say that you can not be what God wants you to be makes God out to be a liar because He is the one that made you, the one that said He knew you while you were in your mother's womb. To say that you can not be what God wants you to be means that God's word is not true as He teaches us that He has equipped us. Understand that it is not what God wants you to be, but it is who He has already designed you to be. When a clockmaker designs a clock it can not over time become a painting. When the furniture maker designs a bed it can over time become the television as it is not the natural order of things. We are to naturally be what God has designed us to be and the simplest way to do that is to stop fighting the natural, divine order of things and allow God to be God so that you can be you!

Righteousness of God

Week 1. Read Psalm 35:27

Let them shout for joy and be glad, who favor my righteous cause; and let them say continually, let the Lord be magnified, who has pleasure in the prosperity of his servant. And my tongue shall speak of your righteousness and of Your praise all the day long.

Sunday's Reflections

Date _____

Journal _____
_____
_____
_____
_____

Monday's Reflections

Date _____

Journal _____
_____
_____
_____
_____

Tuesday's Reflections

Date _____

Journal _____
_____
_____
_____
_____

Wednesday's Reflections

Date _____

Journal _____
_____
_____
_____
_____

Thursday's Reflections

Date_____

Journal _____
_____
_____
_____
_____

Friday's Reflections

Date_____

Journal _____
_____
_____
_____
_____

Saturday's Reflections

Date_____

Journal _____
_____
_____
_____
_____

Week 2. Read Romans 3: 19-26

Now we know that whatever the law says it says to those who are under the law, that every mouth may be stopped, and all the world may become guilty before God. Therefore by the deeds of the law no flesh will be justified in His sight, for by the law is the knowledge of sin. But now the righteousness of God apart from the law is revealed, being witnessed by the Law and the Prophets, even the righteousness of God, through faith in Jesus Christ, to all and on all who believe. For there is no difference; for all have sinned and fall short of the glory of God, being justified freely by his grace through the redemption that is Christ Jesus, whom God set forth as a propitiation by His blood, through faith, to demonstrate His righteousness, because in His forbearance God had passed over the sins that were previously committed, to demonstrate at the present time His righteousness, that He might be just and the justifier of the one who has faith in Jesus.

Sunday's Reflections

Date_____

Journal _____
_____
_____
_____
_____

Monday's Reflections

Date_____

Journal _____
_____
_____
_____
_____

Tuesday's Reflections

Date_____

Journal _____
_____
_____
_____
_____

Wednesday's Reflections

Date_____

Journal _____
_____
_____
_____
_____

Thursday's Reflections

Date_____

Journal _____
_____
_____
_____
_____

Friday's Reflections

Date_____

Journal _____
_____
_____
_____
_____

Saturday's Reflections

Date_____

Journal _____
_____
_____
_____
_____

Week 3. Read Romans 10:1-11

Brethren, my heart's desire and prayer to God for Israel is that they may be saved. For I bear them witness that they have a zeal for God, but not according to knowledge. For they being ignorant of God's righteousness and seeking to establish their own righteousness have not submitted to the righteousness of God. For Christ is the end of the law for righteousness to everyone who believes. For Moses writes about the righteousness which is of the law, "The man who does those things shall live by them." But the righteousness of faith speaks in this way, "Do not say in your heart, 'Who will ascend into heaven?'" (that is, to bring Christ down from above) or, "'Who will descend into the abyss?'" (that is to bring Christ up from the dead) But what does it say? "The word is near you, in your mouth and in your mouth and in your heart." (that is, the word of faith, which we preach): that if you confess with your mouth the Lord Jesus and believe in your heart that God has raised Him from the dead, you will be saved. For with the heart one believes unto righteousness, and with the mouth confession is made into salvation. For the scripture says, "Whoever believes on Him will not be put to shame."

Sunday's Reflections

Date_____

Journal _____
_____
_____
_____
_____

Monday's Reflections

Date_____

Journal _____
_____
_____
_____
_____

Tuesday's Reflections

Date_____

Journal _____
_____
_____
_____
_____

Wednesday's Reflections

Date_____

Journal _____
_____
_____
_____
_____

Thursday's Reflections

Date_____

Journal _____
_____
_____
_____
_____

Friday's Reflections

Date_____

Journal _____
_____
_____
_____
_____

Saturday's Reflections

Date_____

Journal _____
_____
_____
_____
_____

Week 4. Read Psalm 24:4-6

He who has clean hands and a pure heart, who has not lifted up his soul to an idol, nor sworn deceitfully, he shall receive blessings from the Lord, and righteousness from the God of his salvation. This is Jacob the generation of those who seek Him who seek your face.

Sunday's Reflections

Date _____

Journal _____
_____
_____
_____
_____

Monday's Reflections

Date _____

Journal _____
_____
_____
_____
_____

Tuesday's Reflections

Date _____

Journal _____
_____
_____
_____
_____

Wednesday's Reflections

Date _____

Journal _____
_____
_____
_____
_____

Thursday's Reflections

Date_____

Journal _____
_____
_____
_____
_____

Friday's Reflections

Date_____

Journal _____
_____
_____
_____
_____

Saturday's Reflections

Date_____

Journal _____
_____
_____
_____
_____

Week 5. Read Genesis 15:6

And he believes in the Lord, and He accounted it to him for righteousness. Then he said to him, "I am the Lord, who brought you out of Ur of the Chaldeans, to give you this land to inherit it."

Sunday's Reflections

Date_____

Journal _____
_____
_____
_____

Monday's Reflections

Date_____

Journal _____
_____
_____
_____

Tuesday's Reflections

Date_____

Journal _____
_____
_____
_____

Wednesday's Reflections

Date_____

Journal _____
_____
_____
_____

Thursday's Reflections

Date_____

Journal _____
_____
_____
_____
_____

Friday's Reflections

Date_____

Journal _____
_____
_____
_____
_____

Saturday's Reflections

Date_____

Journal _____
_____
_____
_____
_____

Prayer

Father God you said that I can pray your word back to you. You said for with the heart, man believes unto righteousness and with the mouth confession is made unto salvation.

(Now go to the back of the journal and record what God has spoken, the date He spoke it, and when the manifestation of God's promise is revealed; record it in the journal. Go through this process for each week so that the reminder and the remembrance of God's unchanging word is ever before you.)

Knowing God's Will

God desires to be your top priority as the Bible reminds us to seek ye first the kingdom of heaven and everything else will come to you according to God's will. Since God wants to be a priority, He does not keep secrets from you and He does not withhold His will from you. So if you don't know your lover's will, then I challenge you to ask Him. But when you come to Him, come with your heart, mind, and spirit open to His presence and His voice as He begins to speak.

It is not God's plan or desire for us to be in the darkness or to walk in darkness. This is why He consistently sends out the invitation for us to seek his face so that we may know His will. My beloved, I tell you now from the bottom of my heart to stop trying to figure things out on your own. I myself have been guilty of taking something that God has shown me and tried to figure out how to bring it to pass instead of sitting at God's feet a little longer and wait for Him to tell me how it should be brought to pass. We can not add our two cents to any part of God's plan for the Bible reminds us that our ways are not His ways, and His thoughts are not our thoughts. This means that the way God has designed it to be done is not always going to be the way that we would like to do it. But to know His will also means to obey it. Again, I say to trust Him and He will never steer you wrong as you are too precious to Him and He loves you too much!

Knowing God's Will

Week 1. Read Psalm 32:5-8

I acknowledged my sin to You, and my iniquity I have not hidden. I said, "I will confess my transgressions to the Lord," and You forgave the iniquity of my sin. For this cause everyone who is godly shall pray to You. In a time when You may be found; surely in a flood of great water they shall not come near him. You are my hiding place; You shall preserve me from trouble; You shall surround me with songs of deliverance. I will instruct you and teach you in the way you should go; I will guide you with My eye.

Sunday's Reflections

Date_____

Journal _____
_____
_____
_____
_____

Monday's Reflections

Date_____

Journal _____
_____
_____
_____
_____

Tuesday's Reflections

Date_____

Journal _____
_____
_____
_____
_____

Wednesday's Reflections

Date_____

Journal _____
_____
_____
_____
_____

Thursday's Reflections

Date_____

Journal _____
_____
_____
_____
_____

Friday's Reflections

Date_____

Journal _____
_____
_____
_____
_____

Saturday's Reflections

Date_____

Journal _____
_____
_____
_____
_____

Week 2. Read John 10:3-4

To him the doorkeeper opens, and the sheep hear his voice; and he calls his own sheep by name and leads them out. And when he brings out his own sheep, he goes before them; and the sheep follow him, for they know his voice.

Sunday's Reflections

Date _____

Journal _____
_____
_____
_____
_____

Monday's Reflections

Date _____

Journal _____
_____
_____
_____
_____

Tuesday's Reflections

Date _____

Journal _____
_____
_____
_____
_____

Wednesday's Reflections

Date _____

Journal _____
_____
_____
_____
_____

Thursday's Reflections

Date_____

Journal _____
_____
_____
_____
_____

Friday's Reflections

Date_____

Journal _____
_____
_____
_____
_____

Saturday's Reflections

Date_____

Journal _____
_____
_____
_____
_____

Week 3. Read 1 Corinthians 1:29-30

That no flesh should glory in His presence. But of him you are in Christ Jesus who became for us wisdom from God and righteousness and sanctification and redemption.

Sunday's Reflections

Date_____

Journal _____
_____
_____
_____
_____

Monday's Reflections

Date_____

Journal _____
_____
_____
_____
_____

Tuesday's Reflections

Date_____

Journal _____
_____
_____
_____
_____

Wednesday's Reflections

Date_____

Journal _____
_____
_____
_____
_____

Thursday's Reflections

Date_____

Journal _____
_____
_____
_____
_____

Friday's Reflections

Date_____

Journal _____
_____
_____
_____
_____

Saturday's Reflections

Date_____

Journal _____
_____
_____
_____
_____

Week 4. Psalm 16:11 & Psalm 23:3

You will show me the path of life; in your presence is fullness of joy; At your right hand are pleasures forevermore.

He restores my soul; He leads me in the paths of righteousness for His name's sake.

Sunday's Reflections

Date_____

Journal _____
_____
_____
_____
_____

Monday's Reflections

Date_____

Journal _____
_____
_____
_____
_____

Tuesday's Reflections

Date_____

Journal _____
_____
_____
_____
_____

Wednesday's Reflections

Date_____

Journal _____
_____
_____
_____
_____

Thursday's Reflections

Date_____

Journal _____
_____
_____
_____
_____

Friday's Reflections

Date_____

Journal _____
_____
_____
_____
_____

Saturday's Reflections

Date_____

Journal _____
_____
_____
_____
_____

Week 5. Read Ephesians 5:15-17

See then that you walk circumspectly, not as fools but as wise, redeeming the time, because the days are evil. Therefore do not be unwise but understand what the will of the Lord is.

Sunday's Reflections

Date_____

Journal _____
_____
_____
_____
_____

Monday's Reflections

Date_____

Journal _____
_____
_____
_____
_____

Tuesday's Reflections

Date_____

Journal _____
_____
_____
_____
_____

Wednesday's Reflections

Date_____

Journal _____
_____
_____
_____
_____

Thursday's Reflections

Date_____

Journal _____
_____
_____
_____
_____

Friday's Reflections

Date_____

Journal _____
_____
_____
_____
_____

Saturday's Reflections

Date_____

Journal _____
_____
_____
_____
_____

Prayer

Thank you father that Jesus was made unto me wisdom. I ask you to forgive me for my disobedience and create in me a clean heart that I will receive your will as you reveal it to me. No longer will confusion be a part of my life. I am placing my trust in you and will faithfully follow your plan and will for my life with the understanding that my path is being ordered by you. My life is growing unto your ways and my life is becoming clearer.

(Now go to the back of the journal and record what God has spoken, the date He spoke it, and when the manifestation of God's promise is revealed; record it in the journal. Go through this process for each week so that the reminder and the remembrance of God's unchanging word is ever before you.)

Godly Wisdom In The Affairs Of This Life

Trying to make the right decisions are hard sometimes. There is a lot of pressure in trying to ensure that you do everything right. Wouldn't it be great if someone was willing to tell you how to handle different situations and then let you choose which one you wanted to do? Wouldn't it be awesome if there was actually a road map? Well, there is. God is not selfish and it is not His will for us to be blind or confused concerning anything that we have to face or encounter. God will let you know which road you should take when you pray, seek His face, and study His holy word. Then because He is not a dictator, He allows you to make your own decision and you must be willing to live with it

He also has given us a roadmap that outlines not only His instructions, but provides you with examples of those that obeyed and those that disobeyed. There is neither the possibility of failure nor regret when you utilize Godly wisdom. But the keys are God, faith, and obedience. Allow Him to teach you.

When I look back over my life and the mistakes that I made I thank God that He did not condemn me, but He gave me every opportunity to get things right. Now I am not saying that we should do whatever, because we know that God will forgive us. Remember, the whole objective is to experience intimacy with God and to allow Him to be your lover. No one wants to be mistreated or used. Listen to what God tells you, trust in the strength that He gives, but know that if you make a mistake it is not the end. Come to Him, talk to Him, and allow Him to forgive you and then get back on track. Don't ever try to apply logic to anything that God does, for He is not logical….He is God and He loves you!

August

Godly Wisdom in the Affairs of this Life

Week 1. Read Colossians 1:9-10 & Proverbs 2:1-5

For this reason we also, since the day we heard it, do not cease to pray for you, and to ask that you may be filled with the knowledge of His will in all wisdom and spiritual understanding; that you may walk worthy of the Lord, fully pleasing Him, being fruitful in every good work and increasing in the knowledge of God.

My son, if you receive my words, and treasure my commands within you, so that you incline your ear to wisdom, and apply your heart to understanding; yes, if you cry out for discernment, and lift up your voice for understanding, if you seek her as silver, and search for her as for hidden treasures; then you will understand the fear of the Lord, and find the knowledge of God for the Lord gives wisdom; from his mouth come knowledge and understanding.

Sunday's Reflections

Date_____

Journal _____
_____
_____
_____
_____

Monday's Reflections

Date_____

Journal _____
_____
_____
_____
_____

Tuesday's Reflections

Date_____

Journal _____
_____
_____
_____
_____

Wednesday's Reflections

Date_____

Journal _____
_____
_____
_____
_____

Thursday's Reflections

Date_____

Journal _____
_____
_____
_____
_____

Friday's Reflections

Date_____

Journal _____
_____
_____
_____
_____

Saturday's Reflections

Date_____

Journal _____
_____
_____
_____
_____

Week 2. Read Proverbs 4:6-9

Do not forsake her and she will preserve you; Love her, and she will keep you. Wisdom is the principal thing; therefore get wisdom and in all your getting, get understanding. Exalt her and she will promote you. She will bring you honor when you embrace her. She will place on your head an ornament of grace a crown of glory that she will deliver to you.

Sunday's Reflections

Date _____

Journal _____
_____
_____
_____
_____

Monday's Reflections

Date _____

Journal _____
_____
_____
_____
_____

Tuesday's Reflections

Date _____

Journal _____
_____
_____
_____
_____

Wednesday's Reflections

Date _____

Journal _____
_____
_____
_____
_____

Thursday's Reflections

Date_____

Journal _____
_____
_____
_____
_____

Friday's Reflections

Date_____

Journal _____
_____
_____
_____
_____

Saturday's Reflections

Date_____

Journal _____
_____
_____
_____
_____

Week 3. Read Proverbs 3:16-22

Length of days is in her right hand. In her left hand riches and honor. Her ways are ways of pleasantness and all her paths are peace. She is a tree of life to those who take hold of her. And happy are all who retain her. The Lord by wisdom founded the earth; by understanding He established the heavens. By His knowledge the depths were broken up, and clouds drop down the dew. My son let them not depart from your eyes. Keep sound wisdom and discretion so they will be life to your soul and grace to your neck.

Sunday's Reflections

Date_____

Journal _____
_____
_____
_____
_____

Monday's Reflections

Date_____

Journal _____
_____
_____
_____
_____

Tuesday's Reflections

Date_____

Journal _____
_____
_____
_____
_____

Wednesday's Reflections

Date_____

Journal _____
_____
_____
_____
_____

Thursday's Reflections

Date_____

Journal _____
_____
_____
_____
_____

Friday's Reflections

Date_____

Journal _____
_____
_____
_____
_____

Saturday's Reflections

Date_____

Journal _____
_____
_____
_____
_____

Week 4. Read Colossians 2: 1-3

For I want you to know what a great conflict I have for you and those in Laodicea, and for as many as have not seen my face in the flesh, that their hearts may be encouraged, being knit together in love, and attaining to all riches of the full assurance of understanding, to the knowledge of the mystery of God, both of the Father and of Christ, in whom are hidden all the treasures of wisdom and knowledge.

Sunday's Reflections

Date_____

Journal _____
_____
_____
_____
_____

Monday's Reflections

Date_____

Journal _____
_____
_____
_____
_____

Tuesday's Reflections

Date_____

Journal _____
_____
_____
_____
_____

Wednesday's Reflections

Date_____

Journal _____
_____
_____
_____
_____

Thursday's Reflections

Date_____

Journal _____
_____
_____
_____
_____

Friday's Reflections

Date_____

Journal _____
_____
_____
_____
_____

Saturday's Reflections

Date_____

Journal _____
_____
_____
_____
_____

Week 5. Read Psalm 111:10

The fear of the Lord is the beginning of wisdom; a good understanding have all those who do His commandments. His praise endures forever.

Sunday's Reflections

Date_____

Journal _____
_____
_____
_____
_____

Monday's Reflections

Date_____

Journal _____
_____
_____
_____
_____

Tuesday's Reflections

Date_____

Journal _____
_____
_____
_____
_____

Wednesday's Reflections

Date_____

Journal _____
_____
_____
_____
_____

Thursday's Reflections

Date_____

Journal _____
_____
_____
_____
_____

Friday's Reflections

Date_____

Journal _____
_____
_____
_____
_____

Saturday's Reflections

Date_____

Journal _____
_____
_____
_____
_____

Father you said if anyone lacks wisdom let him ask of you who giveth to all men liberally and without reproach, and it shall be given to him. Therefore, I ask in faith, nothing wavering, to be filled with the knowledge of your will in all wisdom and spiritual understanding. Today I incline my ear unto wisdom, and I apply my heart to understanding so that I might receive that which has been freely given unto me.

(Now go to the back of the journal and record what God has spoken, the date He spoke it, and when the manifestation of God's promise is revealed; record it in the journal. Go through this process for each week so that the reminder and the remembrance of God's unchanging word is ever before you.)

Walk In Sanctification

To walk in sanctification means that you don't act like you have been forgiven of your sins, you don't act like you have been washed in the blood of the lamb; you don't act like you have been in the presence of God……you live it; every moment of your life. Whether you are in the store, on your job, with your friends, or with your family you do not turn your sanctification on and off. Sanctification is a cleansing and change that happens on the inside and works its way to the outside, but it can not happen without God. Too many people 'act', it is time to be real!

Your walk is your life, the life that you choose to live. Let your life glorify God as He is the one that sanctifies you and it is up to you to maintain it. Don't allow the demons of your past tell you that you can not be Holy and acceptable unto God because you can. The Bible tells us that if we confess our sins then He is just to forgive us our sins and we can't be forgiven until we have acknowledged what we have through confession of our mouths and asked for forgiveness. Don't allow the demons of your past tell you that the things you have done are too big for God to forgive and too many for Him to love you. The Bible says that God loves us so much that He gave His only son to die for you that you would have the opportunity to be loved by God and live eternally with Him. Remember, the enemy comes to steal, kill, and destroy so silence in the name of Jesus, hold your head up, and walk boldly in sanctification!!

September

Walk in Sanctification

Week 1. Read 2 Corinthians 6: 11-18

O Corinthians! We have spoken openly to you, our heart is wide open. You are not restricted by us, but you are restricted by your own affections. Now in return for the same I speak as to children, you also be open. Do not be unequally yoked together with unbelievers. For what fellowship has righteousness with lawlessness? And what communion has light with darkness? And what accord has Christ with Belial? Or what part has a believer with an unbeliever? And what agreement has the temple of God with idols? For you are the temple of the living God. As God has said, "I will dwell in them and walk among them. I will be their God, and they shall be my people." Therefore, "Come out from among them and be separate," says the Lord. Do not touch what is unclean, and I will receive you. I will be a father to you and you shall be my sons and daughters says the Lord Almighty."

Sunday's Reflections

Date_____

Journal _____
_____
_____
_____
_____

Monday's Reflections

Date_____

Journal _____
_____
_____
_____
_____

Tuesday's Reflections

Date_____

Journal _____
_____
_____
_____
_____

Wednesday's Reflections

Date_____

Journal _____
_____
_____
_____
_____

Thursday's Reflections

Date_____

Journal _____
_____
_____
_____
_____

Friday's Reflections

Date_____

Journal _____
_____
_____
_____
_____

Saturday's Reflections

Date_____

Journal _____
_____
_____
_____
_____

Week 2. Read John 17:14-19

I have given them your word; and the world has hated them because they are not of the world, just as I am not of the world. I do not pray that you should take them out of the world, but that you should keep them from the evil one. They are not of the world just as I am not of the world. Sanctify them by your truth. Your word is truth. As you sent me into the world I also sent them into the world. And for their sake I sanctify myself that they also may be sanctified by the truth.

Sunday's Reflections

Date_____

Journal _____
_____
_____
_____
_____

Monday's Reflections

Date_____

Journal _____
_____
_____
_____
_____

Tuesday's Reflections

Date_____

Journal _____
_____
_____
_____
_____

Wednesday's Reflections

Date_____

Journal _____
_____
_____
_____
_____

Thursday's Reflections

Date_____

Journal _____
_____
_____
_____
_____

Friday's Reflections

Date_____

Journal _____
_____
_____
_____
_____

Saturday's Reflections

Date_____

Journal _____
_____
_____
_____
_____

Week 3. Read Ephesians 4: 20-24

But you have not so learned Christ, if indeed you have heard Him and have been taught by Him as the truth is in Jesus: that you put off, concerning your former conduct, the old man which grows corrupt according to the deceitful lusts, and be renewed in the spirit of your mind, and that you put on the new man which was created according to God, in true righteousness and holiness.

Sunday's Reflections

Date _____

Journal _____
_____
_____
_____
_____

Monday's Reflections

Date _____

Journal _____
_____
_____
_____
_____

Tuesday's Reflections

Date _____

Journal _____
_____
_____
_____
_____

Wednesday's Reflections

Date _____

Journal _____
_____
_____
_____
_____

Thursday's Reflections

Date_____

Journal _____
_____
_____
_____
_____

Friday's Reflections

Date_____

Journal _____
_____
_____
_____
_____

Saturday's Reflections

Date_____

Journal _____
_____
_____
_____
_____

Week 4. Read Isaiah 1: 16-20

Wash yourselves, make yourselves clean; Put away the evil of your doings from before My eyes. Cease to do evil, learn to do good; seek justice, rebuke the oppressor; defend the fatherless, plead for the widow. "Come now and let us reason together" says the Lord. "Though your sins are like scarlet, they shall be as white as snow; Though they are red like crimson, they shall be as wool. If you are willing and obedient, you shall eat the good of the land; but if you refuse and rebel, you shall be devoured by the sword"; For the mouth of the Lord has spoken.

Sunday's Reflections

Date _____

Journal _____
_____
_____
_____
_____

Monday's Reflections

Date _____

Journal _____
_____
_____
_____
_____

Tuesday's Reflections

Date _____

Journal _____
_____
_____
_____
_____

Wednesday's Reflections

Date _____

Journal _____
_____
_____
_____
_____

Thursday's Reflections

Date_____

Journal _____
_____
_____
_____
_____

Friday's Reflections

Date_____

Journal _____
_____
_____
_____
_____

Saturday's Reflections

Date_____

Journal _____
_____
_____
_____
_____

Week 5. Read 2 Timothy 2:19-21

Nevertheless the solid foundation of God stands, having this seal: "The Lord knows those who are His," and, "Let everyone who names the name of Christ depart from iniquity." But in a great house there are not only vessels of gold and silver, but also of wood and clay; some for honor and some for dishonor. Therefore if anyone cleanses himself from the latter, he will be a vessel for honor, sanctified and useful for the Master, prepared for every good work.

Sunday's Reflections

Date_____

Journal _____
_____
_____
_____
_____

Monday's Reflections

Date_____

Journal _____
_____
_____
_____
_____

Tuesday's Reflections

Date_____

Journal _____
_____
_____
_____
_____

Wednesday's Reflections

Date_____

Journal _____
_____
_____
_____
_____

Thursday's Reflections

Date _____

Journal _____
_____
_____
_____
_____

Friday's Reflections

Date _____

Journal _____
_____
_____
_____
_____

Saturday's Reflections

Date _____

Journal _____
_____
_____
_____
_____

Prayer

Father, I confess my sins. You are faithful and just to forgive me of my sins and cleanse me from all unrighteousness. Jesus has been made unto me wisdom, righteousness, sanctification and redemption. I submit myself to you Lord; spirit, soul, and body. I strip myself of my old will so I can have your will for my life.

(Now go to the back of the journal and record what God has spoken, the date He spoke it, and when the manifestation of God's promise is revealed; record it in the journal. Go through this process for each week so that the reminder and the remembrance of God's unchanging word is ever before you.)

Watch What You Say

We all remember vividly how we were hurt in previous relationships, whether they were family relationships, friend relationships, or more than friend relationships. We also remember how because of our own hurt; we lashed out at someone else who really did not deserve it. God lets us know that there is power in what we say or do not say. When we have the opportunity to encourage we should do it, but we should be careful not to let negative emotion come from our mouths. The God that you have now committed yourself to is constantly encouraging you, constantly giving His love to you, and since we endeavor to be like Him, we must do the same. Just like you chose life when you decided to let God into your heart; it is now time to choose to speak life into yourself and into others.

You may be thinking right now that you don't know what to say or sometimes you are at a loss for words. That is when you need to pick up your Bible and begin speaking the Word of God into yourself and into others around you. The Word of God is the truth and it must be fulfilled. The one thing that the enemy can not argue with are the Words that proceed out of the mouth of God for He knows that they contain a power that he can not harness and can not control. The only thing that the enemy can do is try and stop you from speaking them. Don't allow Him to steal any moment of this experience from you. Treat the Word of God as personal love letters that God Himself wrote to you and keep those words in your heart so that in times of trouble and distress you can recall them and find strength in them.

October

Watch What You Say

Week 1. Read Proverbs 18:20

Death and life are in the power of the tongue, and those who love it will eat its fruit.

Sunday's Reflections

Date_____

Journal _____
_____
_____
_____
_____

Monday's Reflections

Date_____

Journal _____
_____
_____
_____
_____

Tuesday's Reflections

Date_____

Journal _____
_____
_____
_____
_____

Wednesday's Reflections

Date_____

Journal _____
_____
_____
_____
_____

Thursday's Reflections

Date_____

Journal _____
_____
_____
_____
_____

Friday's Reflections

Date_____

Journal _____
_____
_____
_____
_____

Saturday's Reflections

Date_____

Journal _____
_____
_____
_____
_____

Week 2. Read Colossians 3:16-17

Let the word of Christ dwell in you richly in all wisdom, teaching and admonishing one another in psalms and hymns and spiritual songs, singing with grace in your hearts to the Lord. And whatever you do in word or deed, do all in the name of the Lord Jesus giving thanks to God the Father through him.

Sunday's Reflections

Date_____

Journal _____
_____
_____
_____
_____

Monday's Reflections

Date_____

Journal _____
_____
_____
_____
_____

Tuesday's Reflections

Date_____

Journal _____
_____
_____
_____
_____

Wednesday's Reflections

Date_____

Journal _____
_____
_____
_____
_____

Thursday's Reflections

Date_____

Journal _____
_____
_____
_____
_____

Friday's Reflections

Date_____

Journal _____
_____
_____
_____
_____

Saturday's Reflections

Date_____

Journal _____
_____
_____
_____
_____

Week 3. Read Proverbs 21:23 & James 3:6-10

Whoever guards his mouth and tongue keeps his soul from troubles. And the tongue is a fire, in a world of iniquity. The tongue is so set among our members that it defiles the whole body, and sets on fire the course of nature; and it is set on fire by hell. For every kind of beast, bird, reptile, and creature of the sea is tamed and has been tamed by mankind. But no man can tame the tongue. It is an unruly evil, full of deadly poison. With it we bless our God and Father, and with it we curse men, who have been made in similitude of God. Out of the same mouth proceed blessing and cursing my brethren those things ought not to be so.

Sunday's Reflections

Date_____

Journal _____
_____
_____
_____

Monday's Reflections

Date_____

Journal _____
_____
_____
_____

Tuesday's Reflections

Date_____

Journal _____
_____
_____
_____

Wednesday's Reflections

Date_____

Journal _____
_____
_____
_____

Thursday's Reflections

Date_____

Journal _____
_____
_____
_____
_____

Friday's Reflections

Date_____

Journal _____
_____
_____
_____
_____

Saturday's Reflections

Date_____

Journal _____
_____
_____
_____
_____

Week 4. Read Proverbs 8:6-8

Listen for I will speak of excellent things and from the opening of my lips will come right things. For my mouth will speak truth. Wickedness is an abomination to my lips. All the words of my mouth are with righteousness.

Sunday's Reflections

Date_____

Journal _____
_____
_____
_____
_____

Monday's Reflections

Date_____

Journal _____
_____
_____
_____
_____

Tuesday's Reflections

Date_____

Journal _____
_____
_____
_____
_____

Wednesday's Reflections

Date_____

Journal _____
_____
_____
_____
_____

Thursday's Reflections

Date_____

Journal _____
_____
_____
_____
_____

Friday's Reflections

Date_____

Journal _____
_____
_____
_____
_____

Saturday's Reflections

Date_____

Journal _____
_____
_____
_____
_____

Week 5. Read John 6: 61-63

When Jesus knew in himself that his disciples complained about this, He said to them, "Does this offend you? What then if you should see the Son of Man ascend where he was before? It is the spirit who gives life, the flesh profits nothing. The words that I speak to you are spirit and they are life."

Sunday's Reflections

Date_____

Journal _____
_____
_____
_____
_____

Monday's Reflections

Date_____

Journal _____
_____
_____
_____
_____

Tuesday's Reflections

Date_____

Journal _____
_____
_____
_____
_____

Wednesday's Reflections

Date_____

Journal _____
_____
_____
_____
_____

Thursday's Reflections

Date _____

Journal _____
_____
_____
_____
_____

Friday's Reflections

Date _____

Journal _____
_____
_____
_____
_____

Saturday's Reflections

Date _____

Journal _____
_____
_____
_____
_____

Prayer

Father, your words are top priority to me. They are spirit and life. I let the Word dwell in me richly in all wisdom. The ability of God is released within me by the words of my mouth and by the Word of God. I speak your words out of my mouth. They are alive in me; you are alive and working in me. So, I can boldly decree my words of faith, words of power, words of love, and words of life. They produce good things in our life and in the lives of others because I choose your words for my life and your will for my life in Jesus name, Amen.

(Now go to the back of the journal and record what God has spoken, the date He spoke it, and when the manifestation of God's promise is revealed; record it in the journal. Go through this process for each week so that the reminder and the remembrance of God's unchanging word is ever before you.)

Walk In The Word

To walk in the Word of God is to walk with God. Believing in Him, trusting in Him, and allowing Him to be who He needs to be in your life. It means to live out your days with the Father, and not putting any boundaries or limitations on Him. It means accepting everything that flows out of Him and allowing it to penetrate your very being. It means allowing these intimate moments to continue through eternity.

This is only the beginning of what is yet to come. The end of this journal does not mean the end of your experience for the truth of the matter is that the journey never ends and I mean never. When you reside with the Father in Heaven, you will still be experiencing the awesome of who He is and the love that He has to give and wants to give. He does not turn on and off, but His light and His love shines for all eternity so walk in His Word and basque in His love!

November

Walk in the Word

Week 1. Read Psalm 91:1-4 & Psalm 119:105

He who dwells in the secret place of the most high shall abide under the shadow of the Almighty. I will say of the Lord, He is my refuge and my fortress, my God, in Him I will trust. Surely He shall deliver you from the snare of fowler. And from the perilous pestilence He shall cover you with His feathers and under His wings you shall take refuge.

Your word is a lamp to my feet and a light to my path.

Sunday's Reflections

Date_____

Journal _____
_____
_____
_____
_____

Monday's Reflections

Date_____

Journal _____
_____
_____
_____
_____

Tuesday's Reflections

Date_____

Journal _____
_____
_____
_____
_____

Wednesday's Reflections

Date_____

Journal _____
_____
_____
_____
_____

Thursday's Reflections

Date_____

Journal _____
_____
_____
_____
_____

Friday's Reflections

Date_____

Journal _____
_____
_____
_____
_____

Saturday's Reflections

Date_____

Journal _____
_____
_____
_____
_____

Week 2. Read Joshua 1:8

This book of the law shall not depart from your mouth but you shall meditate in it day and night; that you may observe to do according to all that is written in it. For then you will make your way prosperous and then you will have good success.

Sunday's Reflections

Date _____

Journal _____
_____
_____
_____
_____

Monday's Reflections

Date _____

Journal _____
_____
_____
_____
_____

Tuesday's Reflections

Date _____

Journal _____
_____
_____
_____
_____

Wednesday's Reflections

Date _____

Journal _____
_____
_____
_____
_____

Thursday's Reflections

Date_____

Journal _____
_____
_____
_____
_____

Friday's Reflections

Date_____

Journal _____
_____
_____
_____
_____

Saturday's Reflections

Date_____

Journal _____
_____
_____
_____
_____

Week 3. Read John 1:1-5

In the beginning was the Word, and the Word was with God, and the Word was God. He was in the beginning with God. All things were made through Him, and without Him nothing was made that was made. In Him was life, and the life was the light of men. And the light shines in the darkness, and the darkness did not comprehend it.

Sunday's Reflections

Date_____

Journal _____
_____
_____
_____
_____

Monday's Reflections

Date_____

Journal _____
_____
_____
_____
_____

Tuesday's Reflections

Date_____

Journal _____
_____
_____
_____
_____

Wednesday's Reflections

Date_____

Journal _____
_____
_____
_____
_____

Thursday's Reflections

Date_____

Journal _____
_____
_____
_____
_____

Friday's Reflections

Date_____

Journal _____
_____
_____
_____
_____

Saturday's Reflections

Date_____

Journal _____
_____
_____
_____
_____

Week 4. Read 1 Peter 1:22-23

Since you have purified your souls in obeying the truth through the Spirit in sincere love of the brethren, love one another fervently with a pure heart, having been born again, not of corruptible seed but incorruptible through the word of God which lives and abides forever.

Sunday's Reflections

Date_____

Journal _____
_____
_____
_____
_____

Monday's Reflections

Date_____

Journal _____
_____
_____
_____
_____

Tuesday's Reflections

Date_____

Journal _____
_____
_____
_____
_____

Wednesday's Reflections

Date_____

Journal _____
_____
_____
_____
_____

Thursday's Reflections

Date_____

Journal _____
_____
_____
_____
_____

Friday's Reflections

Date_____

Journal _____
_____
_____
_____
_____

Saturday's Reflections

Date_____

Journal _____
_____
_____
_____
_____

Week 5. Read 2 Corinthians 10:3-5

For though we walk in the flesh, we do not war according to the flesh. For the weapons of our warfare are not carnal but mighty in God for pulling down strongholds, casting down arguments and every high that exalts itself against the knowledge of God, bringing every thought into captivity to the obedience of Christ.

Sunday's Reflections

Date_____

Journal _____
_____
_____
_____
_____

Monday's Reflections

Date_____

Journal _____
_____
_____
_____
_____

Tuesday's Reflections

Date_____

Journal _____
_____
_____
_____
_____

Wednesday's Reflections

Date_____

Journal _____
_____
_____
_____
_____

Thursday's Reflections

Date_____

Journal _____
_____
_____
_____
_____

Friday's Reflections

Date_____

Journal _____
_____
_____
_____
_____

Saturday's Reflections

Date_____

Journal _____
_____
_____
_____
_____

Prayer

Father God you have sent your word forth into my heart. I let it dwell in me richly in wisdom. I meditate in it day and night so that I may diligently act on it. The incorruptible seed, the living word, the word of truth is abiding in my spirit. That seed is growing mightily in me now producing your nature and your life. It is my counsel, my shield, my buckler, my powerful weapon in battle. Your word is a lamp to my feet and a light to my path. It makes my way plain before me. I do not stumble for my steps are ordered in the word.

(Now go to the back of the journal and record what God has spoken, the date He spoke it, and when the manifestation of God's promise is revealed; record it in the journal. Go through this process for each week so that the reminder and the remembrance of God's unchanging word is ever before you.)

What The Blood of Jesus Can Do

The blood of Jesus can do anything but fail at its purpose. The blood will wash those who want to be washed, protect those who want to be protected, purify, sanctify, and the list goes on and on. But you can not call on the blood until you have accepted the Son of God, Jesus Christ, as your personal savior. You have to believe in its power and believe in its source.

By now God has shown you the things that are hindering the intimate relationship that He desires to exist between Him and you. He has shown what and who needs to be removed from your life and what you need to cling to. He has shown you where you are broken and how He wants to restore unto all that the enemy has taken and also that which has been given to the enemy. But it can not happen without the blood of Jesus. Everything you pray must be prayed by the blood of Jesus and when you need strength it is done through the blood and the things on the inside of you that need to be healed or restored will be done when you decree it by the blood of Jesus.

Now is where your real journey will begin. The Word of God declares that no one can get to the Father except through the Son. Plead the blood of Jesus over your life and the life of your family right now. Cry out unto God and let the enemy know that you have had enough. Let him know that by the blood of Jesus you are free for the Word of God declares that whom the Son makes free is free indeed. Don't allow anything to come in between you and your intimacy with God for the experience is no where near over. Know that you are loved, you are wanted, you are cherished, you are blessed, and you are forgiven!!!

December

What the Blood of Jesus Can Do

Week 1. Read Hebrews 9: 11-14

But Christ came as High Priest of the good things to come with the greater and more perfect tabernacle not made with hands, that is, not of this creation. Not with the blood of goat and calves, but with His own blood, he entered the Most Holy Place once for all, having obtained eternal redemption. For if the blood of bulls and goats and the ashes of a heifer, sprinkling the unclean, sanctifies for the purifying of the flesh, how much more shall the blood of Christ, who through the eternal Spirit offered Himself without spot to God, shall cleanse your conscience from dead works to serve the living God? And for this reason He is the Mediator of the new covenant, by means of death, for the redemption of the transgressions under the first covenant, that those who are called may receive the promise of the eternal inheritance.

Sunday's Reflections

Date_____

Journal _____
_____
_____
_____
_____

Monday's Reflections

Date_____

Journal _____
_____
_____
_____
_____

Tuesday's Reflections

Date_____

Journal _____
_____
_____
_____
_____

Wednesday's Reflections

Date_____

Journal _____
_____
_____
_____
_____

Thursday's Reflections

Date_____

Journal _____
_____
_____
_____
_____

Friday's Reflections

Date_____

Journal _____
_____
_____
_____
_____

Saturday's Reflections

Date_____

Journal _____
_____
_____
_____
_____

Week 2. Read 1 Corinthians 6:19-20

Or do you know that your body is the temple of the Holy Spirit who is in you whom you have from God and you are not your own? For you were bought at a price therefore glorify God in your body and in your spirit which are God.

Sunday's Reflections

Date_____

Journal _____
_____
_____
_____
_____

Monday's Reflections

Date_____

Journal _____
_____
_____
_____
_____

Tuesday's Reflections

Date_____

Journal _____
_____
_____
_____
_____

Wednesday's Reflections

Date_____

Journal _____
_____
_____
_____
_____

Thursday's Reflections

Date_____

Journal _____
_____
_____
_____
_____

Friday's Reflections

Date_____

Journal _____
_____
_____
_____
_____

Saturday's Reflections

Date_____

Journal _____
_____
_____
_____
_____

Week 3. Read Hebrews 13:20

Now may the God of peace who brought up our Lord Jesus from the dead, that great Shepherd of the sheep, through the blood of the everlasting covenant make you complete in every good work to do His will, working in you what is well pleasing in His sight through Jesus Christ, to whom be glory forever and ever, Amen.

Sunday's Reflections

Date_____

Journal _____
_____
_____
_____
_____

Monday's Reflections

Date_____

Journal _____
_____
_____
_____
_____

Tuesday's Reflections

Date_____

Journal _____
_____
_____
_____
_____

Wednesday's Reflections

Date_____

Journal _____
_____
_____
_____
_____

Thursday's Reflections

Date_____

Journal _____
_____
_____
_____
_____

Friday's Reflections

Date_____

Journal _____
_____
_____
_____
_____

Saturday's Reflections

Date_____

Journal _____
_____
_____
_____
_____

Week 4. Read 1 John 1:7

But if we walk in the light as He is in the light, we have fellowship with one another, and the blood of Jesus Christ His Son cleanses us from all sin. If we say that we have no sin we deceive ourselves and the truth is not in us. If we confess our sins, He is faithful and just to forgive us our sins and to cleanse us from all unrighteousness. If we say that we have not sinned we make him a liar and His word is not in us.

Sunday's Reflections

Date_____

Journal _____
_____
_____
_____
_____

Monday's Reflections

Date_____

Journal _____
_____
_____
_____
_____

Tuesday's Reflections

Date_____

Journal _____
_____
_____
_____
_____

Wednesday's Reflections

Date_____

Journal _____
_____
_____
_____
_____

Thursday's Reflections

Date_____

Journal _____
_____
_____
_____
_____

Friday's Reflections

Date_____

Journal _____
_____
_____
_____
_____

Saturday's Reflections

Date_____

Journal _____
_____
_____
_____
_____

Week 5. Leviticus 17:11

For the life of the flesh is in the blood, and I have given it to you upon the alter to make atonement for your souls; for it is the blood that makes atonement for the soul.

Prayer

Father I come in the name of Jesus to plead His blood over my life and on all that belongs to me, and over all which you have made me a steward. I plead the blood of Jesus on the portals of my mind, my body, my emotions, and my will. I believe that I am protected by the blood of the lamb, which gives me access to the Holy of Holies. I plead the blood on all those to whom you have given me in this life. Lord you have said that the life of the flesh is in the blood. Thank you for this blood that cleanses us from sin and sealed the new covenant of which I am a partaker.

(Now go to the back of the journal and record what God has spoken, the date He spoke it, and when the manifestation of God's promise is revealed; record it in the journal. Go through this process for each week so that the reminder and the remembrance of God's unchanging word is ever before you.)

Sunday's Reflections

Date_____

Journal _____
_____
_____
_____
_____

Monday's Reflections

Date_____

Journal _____
_____
_____
_____
_____

Tuesday's Reflections

Date_____

Journal _____
_____
_____
_____
_____

Wednesday's Reflections

Date_____

Journal _____
_____
_____
_____
_____

Thursday's Reflections

Date_____

Journal _____
_____
_____
_____
_____

Friday's Reflections

Date_____

Journal _____
_____
_____
_____
_____

Saturday's Reflections

Date_____

Journal _____
_____
_____
_____
_____

Notes

Notes

Christian Calendar

Christian Church Year

The Season of Advent: The first season of the liturgical year begins four Sundays before Christmas and ends on Christmas Eve. Historically observed as a "fast", its purpose focuses on preparation for the coming Christ and the colors are purple/violet.

The Season of Christmas: Christmastide begins the evening of Christmas Eve (December 24) and ends on the Feast of the Epiphany on January 6. Christmas Day itself is December 25. The 12-day length of the Christmas season gives rise to "The Twelve Days of Christmas"; which begin on Christmas Day, instead of ending on it. The colors used are white and gold.

The Season of Epiphany: It extends from January 6th until Ash Wednesday, which begins the season of Lent and the color is green.

The Season of Lent: Lent is a major fast taken by the Church to prepare for Easter. It begins on Ash Wednesday and ends on Palm Sunday, at the beginning of Holy Week. There are forty days of Lent, counting from Ash Wednesday through Palm Sunday and the color is purple/violet.

Holy Week: The days between Palm Sunday and Holy Saturday before Easter are known as Holy Week. These days observe the events in the life of Jesus from the entry into Jerusalem through the crucifixion and burial. Palm Sunday is sometimes called Passion Sunday because of the tragic events of the week to come.

The Season of Easter: Easter is the celebration of Jesus' resurrection. The date of Easter varies from year to year, according to a lunar-calendar based dating system. The Easter season extends from the Easter Vigil through Pentecost Sunday and the color is white.
Pentecost: the fiftieth day after Easter Sunday, which corresponds to the tenth day after Ascension Thursday. It commemorates the descent of the Holy Spirit upon the Apostles and the followers of Jesus on that day, as described in the Book of Acts, Chapter 2 and the color is red.

Kingdomtide: start the season on the Sunday on or nearest August 31, which gives Kingdomtide 13 Sundays every year; in some places, Kingdomtide is commenced on the last Sunday in August, giving the season 13 Sundays in some years and 14 in others. It stresses charity and assistance to the poor and the color is green.

I hope you enjoyed this Jouney and that it filled you heart with hope. Continue to persue your personal relationship with the Living Christ, he is your friend and he loves you more than anything. Talk to him daily and allow him to guide you, and use this journal year after year. This journal is a place to reflect and meditate on the things he has shown you throughout your life.

May God Bless You and Keep You your whole life through.

Teresa Johnson